THE JOURNAL

*Discover the Voice of
Your Inner Musical Muse*

A Journaling Course and Daytimer System
For Musicians

by Ami Sarasvati
Cover art and branding graphics
by Brenda Girolamo

Get Your Free Gifts!

As a heartfelt thank you, valuable downloads and resources are available to support you on your Musician's Heart Journey.

musiciansheartjourney.com

Copyright © 2021 Ami Sarasvati. All rights reserved.

Ami's special thanks to:

The Music for People organization, Music for Healing and Transitions Program, all the music teachers throughout my life, Concord Hospital (Concord, NH) for the remarkable experiences as a Certified Music Practitioner, and my Mom who took me to piano lessons every Friday afternoon as a child.

Edited by Pam LaCroix

Cover art and branding graphics by Brenda Girolamo

First Printing: September 2021

ISBN: 978-1-7371632-0-6

Table of Contents

Preface 5

SECTION ONE
Illuminating the Path 6
The Journey Inward 8
Musical Breath Meditation 12
Future Musical Self Meditation 15
A Paradigm Shift 21
Releasing Meditation at the Crossroad 26
Musical Library Meditation 28
Create Your Musical Timeline 34
Make Your Musical Wishlist 38
Map Your Journey: Create a Musical Vision Board 42
Learn to Use the Compass (Weekly Daytimer) 46
Learn to Use the Magnifying Glass (Reflection Questions) . . . 53
Learn to Use the Open Pages 56

SECTION TWO 60
52 weeks of the Compass, the Magnifying Glass,
and two Open Pages between weeks

SECTION THREE 272
Additional blank pages for your musical musing

Testimonials

"Musical Inspiration and Journaling"

As a child, I was a music lover. We could not afford an instrument so I sang in the church and school choirs. As an adult with adult children, I am now teaching myself how to play the keyboard. The tools in Musicians Heart Journey are teaching me how to relax and think about what music means to me. I am learning through meditating to allow my entire being to become involved in the process of learning to play and write music. This is a great book for anyone who loves music and journaling. From my perspective, anyone who desires to release anxiety, tension or stress can learn how to focus and explore what is within.

— *Rebecca Pinkney Thomas*

"A wonderful resource for inspiration and focus!"

I especially like the tools of the Compass and Magnifying Glass to create reflection on how you have spent your musical week and where you might want to go. I am excited about using this method to integrate my musical interests and help me to choose paths for their growth.

— *Susan M Beers*

"The Artist's Way for Musicians!"

The Musician's Heart Journey Journaling Course reminded me of Julia Cameron's The Artist's Way designed specifically for musicians. This provides a number of very practical tools and techniques for finding your musical muse and embarking upon your personal musician's journey of discovery and creativity. A particularly valuable resource if you find yourself stuck in a rut, bored, uninspired, out of ideas or frustrated at where you currently find yourself as a musician. This work will get you out of that rut, inspired and filled with musical creativity and action!

— *Calico Pete*

"If you are a musician and love journaling this book is for you!"

I loved the idea of a book that combines my love of journaling with my musical background. The book has many great ways to explore your inner musical muse. In the past, I have written about my musical beginnings, current activities, and plans for the future. However, I have never come across the idea of using meditations and writing prompts to begin journaling. I have always liked reading back on what I wrote. This method gives you the opportunity to do just that and set goals for the coming week. I am looking forward to seeing my musical vision unfold.

— *Katrina Curdy*

"Engaging and Inspiring"

The author touches on so many key elements in her book. The meditations are engaging and connect us to that creative aspect in each of us that is just waiting to be explored and shared. If you played a musical instrument in your younger days and feel an inner stirring to start up again, this is an excellent way to engage. I highly recommend this book for beginners and seasoned musicians.

— *Suzanne*

Preface

Musician's Heart Journey is best read in order.

This course is an interactive journey of meditations, visualization tools, and inspiring journal prompts so you can tap into your true musical passion revealed by the voice of your inner musical muse. This voice comes in the form of words, paragraphs, images, inklings, urges, and surges. You are compassionately and creatively escorted on this journey every step of the way in discovering and developing this important inner resource.

The accessory books enhance your journey. You can also use a plain notebook or an electronic device. Use the writing method of your choice. Give yourself plenty of time and room to further explore insights that come when doing this work.

The case examples are sketches of previous students, friends, and colleagues. Identifying characteristics have been modified so that identities are protected.

Musician's Heart Journey is a place of discovery and exploration for all musicians seeking to get in touch with their inner musical muse. It is a structured journaling course as well as a daytimer for musicians. This journal offers powerful tools which the reader can use for a lifetime. Regardless of musical experience, the method presented on these pages is intended to illuminate the next step on your unique and authentic Musician's Heart Journey.

Resources Available

Two accessory paperback books are available for this work. For future work, accessory books are available in small, medium, and large sizes. Links to all books and downloads are on **musiciansheartjourney.com**.

Look for:
Musician's Heart Journey: Companion Journal,
Musician's Heart Journey Weekly Daytimer, and
Musician's Heart Journey: The Journal - ebook format

You can also download, print, and assemble these pages. FREE downloads of the Compass, the Magnifying Glass, and Open Pages are available at **musiciansheartjourney.com**.

Welcome to the Musician's Heart Journey

Illuminating the Path

The Musician's Heart Journey is a course in self-discovery for musicians who enjoy journaling and who desire to tune in to the voice of the inner musical muse—the voice that offers constant and authentic guidance on one's unique musical path. This course provides a map and practical tools used in conjunction with the writing method of your choice. The creation of Musician's Heart Journey is a conduit through which you can develop an essential internal resource so that your unique musical passion can manifest.

Tools used for this work:

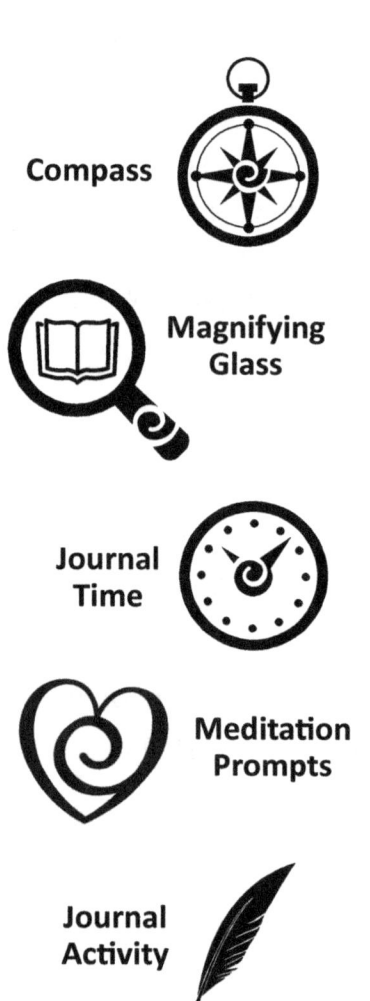

Using a method of deep listening, journaling, and reviewing, you will access inner guidance to illuminate the next step on your musical path.

On this journey, your writing is a private endeavor. You can journal in peace, knowing that your words are for your eyes only. In a quiet and private space, you have a safe place to do what you love to do: write, explore, dream, and discover yourself on the page.

Inner whisperings and impressions come to you in the form of words, paragraphs, even pages, as well as shapes, drawings, inklings, urges, and surges. These impressions provide insight on how to take the next step on your unique musical path.

> *"Dance like nobody's watching; love like you've never been hurt. Sing like nobody's listening; live like it's heaven on earth."*
>
> **– ATTRIBUTED TO SEVERAL PEOPLE**

The Musician's Heart Journey adds to this liberating quote and claims your complete privacy on this journey inviting you to *journal like no one but you will ever read these words*.

Enjoy journaling freely and with no regard to order, syntax, or making any sense—think stream of consciousness. Guided journal prompts are provided with the intention of inviting your musical muse to show you the way. This method of journaling and reviewing can reveal a surprising mosaic of your musicality.

The Journey Inward

This is a journey into your musician's heart. Through guided journaling and other activities, the voice of your musical muse appears before your eyes through your own writing and drawing.

Method of journaling used in this course:

1. Going Inward with a Musical Breath Meditation

2. Listening, Witnessing, and Receiving

3. Journaling on What Comes to You (writing prompts provided)

4. Reading, Reviewing, and Reflecting to Illuminate the Path Forward

The following few pages describe these four steps. There is no need to do these steps now. This is an overview of the process, so you get an idea of how these steps work.

1. Going Inward with a Musical Breath Meditation

You will begin by quieting yourself as you transition from being in a doing-and-thinking mode into a listening-and-receiving mode. A musical breath mantra is used as a vehicle to go inward. The mantras give your mind a simple focal point to help you move into a quiet inner space. Going inward is an essential process of this method so that your inspirations and insights come from your inner self and not primarily from external influences. This simple mantra is coordinated with a breathing pattern.

2. Listening, Witnessing, and Receiving

As you allow yourself to sink deeper into a quiet place within, you may receive words, images, urges, flashes, feelings, or inklings. You are invited to simply stay in a receptive mode and observe what shows up or comes to you. There is nothing to figure out now.

"Art is not about thinking something up.
It's about the opposite—getting something down...
If we're trying to think something up, we are straining to reach for
something that is beyond our grasp. When we get something down,
there is no strain. We're not doing, we're getting. Instead of reaching for
inventions, we are engaged in listening. Art is an act
of tuning in and dropping down the well."

– JULIA CAMERON, *THE ARTIST'S WAY*

In this inner landscape, the veil between your everyday existence and the field of limitless possibilities is thin. Receive what comes to you with neutrality. Simply notice everything.

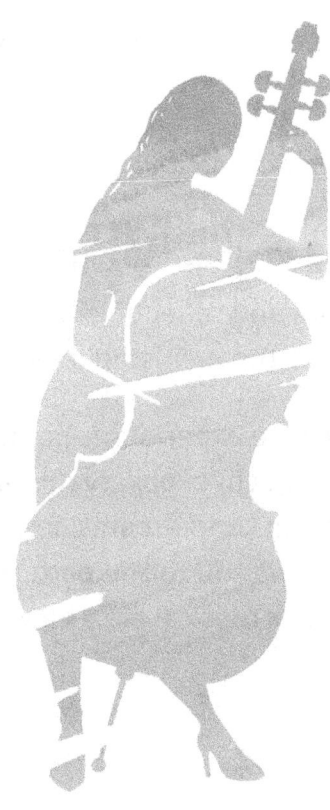

3. Journal on What Comes to You (writing prompts provided)

Have you ever had the experience, while journaling, that you were trying to keep up with the flow of thoughts rushing through your heart and hands, almost like you were taking dictation? This experience validates that you are in the receptive state and on the right path. The following example is offered to illustrate this process.

Robert is a 57-year-old software engineer who has played percussion instruments since he was in his twenties. He secretly yearns to learn a new instrument, the one that causes a revolution in his heart, but feels confined by his established percussion skills. He explores his musical yearning as he pours his heart out onto the page.

Robert writes:

> *I get this image like I'm in a daydream. I'm at some sort of music camp, playing cello with an ability I've only dreamed about. My hands know the instrument, the music, the nuances. It is effortless and ecstatic. But I've played drums for 30 years now. I'm the percussionist with my music friends, but when I hear music played on the cello, I feel my heart pound stronger. There is a deep connection within me to the "other" instrument. How can I possibly tell my wife I want to take up a different instrument? I make good money playing gigs with the drums. Would I even have time to learn a new instrument? I wonder how it would feel to be able to play the cello really well.*

Journaling in this way reveals your inner sparks and invites your exploration.

4. Reading, Reviewing, and Reflecting to Illuminate the Path Forward

The final step is reading what you just wrote and reflecting, in writing, upon any insights that come to you. This important step illuminates the next step on your musical journey.

Your journaling is an account of your subjective experience, no more, no less. As you read what you just wrote, you switch over to a more objective, observant, and detached perspective. Insights show up in your journaling. Your truths and dreams literally appear before your eyes on the pages. Writing them down on paper allows you to see patterns. Uncensored and completely private, you begin to get a perspective of your musical life as a whole as well as where you are on the path right now.

Discovering your true musical interests may take you in unexpected directions. This step is all about quieting yourself and listening deeply as you tap into unlimited possibilities.

Now that the four-step process has been described, it is time to experience it for yourself.

Think of this part of the journey as Base Camp. Take as much time as you need on the meditations and journal prompts that follow. They are not meant to be done all at once. Allow yourself to integrate at your own pace. Experience these powerful meditations and notice what comes with each one.

Be sure to give yourself plenty of time, ideally without interruption. Set yourself up in a quiet and private space, if possible, so that you can fully engage in this process.

Musical Breath Meditation

 This meditation has been recorded by the author and can be downloaded for an audible experience. Go to musiciansheartjourney.com to sign up to receive this free gift as well as other valuable resources.

For this meditation, have this Journal or another writing medium of your choice nearby, but not in your hands or on your body.

 Come to a seated position with both feet on the ground. Sit with a comfortably straight spine. You can be lying down if necessary, but it may be easy to fall asleep that way. Explore what posture works best for you.

Put everything else down and place your hands, palms facing up, on your lap, in a receptive, relaxed manner. You will journal after the meditation.

It is recommended that you breathe through your nose during the meditations. If you cannot, it is okay. You may also choose to put the tip of your tongue on the roof of your mouth as you meditate. [pause]

Begin to relax your body. Bring your focus to your breath. Without changing anything or judging anything, just notice your breath—the rise and fall of your breath. Notice your breathing at this moment. Observe your body and your breath. [pause]

Bring your attention to where your body is supported. If you are on a chair, notice where your body touches the chair. Feel your body fully supported. Now bring your attention to your feet and notice where they are resting on the ground.

Continue to quiet yourself by slowing and deepening your breath. Sink into a quiet space within. Feel your breath moving through your body. Tune in to the beating of your heart.

Allow yourself to go a little deeper into a quiet space within. Begin to inhale to the count of three [pause] and exhale a little more slowly to the count of four. [pause]

Use this breathing pattern to transition into a relaxed and receptive mode. This is not a time for analysis. Let any thoughts or concerns that come up in your mind pass by like clouds passing across the sky. [pause]

The next step is to add musical words to the breathing pattern. This is done silently and subtly. Let the words ride on your breath, going in and out.

For a slow count of three…

Quietly breathe in as you focus on the three syllables "Mu-si-cal."

And then to a slow count of four…

Breathe out as you focus on the four syllables "I-den-ti-ty."

Go a little deeper into the stillness by repeating this mantra as the words silently ride in and out on your breath. [pause]

You can expand the practice by pausing at the top and the bottom of your breath. Honor the natural rhythm of your body.

Allow your breath to ride on the words as you inhale "musical" and exhale "identity."

Notice whatever comes to you. Meditate in this quiet space for a few minutes. [long pause]

In a moment, we will bring this meditation to a gradual close, but for a little longer, dwell in the quiet space deep within. [pause]

Know that this musical breath mantra is yours for life, to take you deep within, anytime.

Gently deepen your breath. Begin to wiggle your toes. Lightly rub your hands together. Perhaps even brush them over your face and back over your head. Take a deep breath and exhale with a releasing sigh. Come back fully to the present space and time. [pause]

Give yourself a few minutes to integrate as you come to closure with this meditation. Continue to take a few more long, slow, deep breaths to help you integrate this experience. [pause]

 It is time to journal.

There are two steps left.

First, you will journal on your experience of the meditation. Trust any impressions, flashes, words, or anything else that comes.

Journal for five minutes or more, then find a good stopping place. You may begin now.
[long pause to journal]

The final step is to read what you just wrote from a curious and neutral perspective. After you have read your new journal entry, journal on what you notice about it. Feel free to use the pages in the back (Section Three), or your Companion Journal, to respond to the following prompts:

What occurs to you about your journal entry?

Do you notice any themes or patterns?

Are there any surprises?

Remember, your journaling is for your eyes only, so allow yourself to fully express your deepest desires and curiosities on the page. This final step of reflective journaling is often fruitful and revealing. Staying in a quiet and receptive space, let it flow through you.

🕐   Take one more minute to journal.

Is there anything else to record at this moment while it is fresh in your mind?

It is time to bring your writing to a good stopping place for now.

This is the end of the Musical Breath Meditation.

You've taken a new step on your Musician's Heart Journey. More insights will likely come to you about this experience. You can return to your journal anytime to explore and develop this work.

Future Musical Self Meditation

This meditation has been recorded by the author and can be downloaded for an audible experience. Go to musiciansheartjourney.com to sign up to receive this free gift as well as other valuable resources.

Come to a seated position with both feet on the ground. Sit with a comfortably straight spine. You can be lying down if necessary, but it may be easy to fall asleep that way. Explore what posture works best for you.

Have this Journal or another writing medium of your choice nearby, but not in your hands or on your body. Put everything else down and place your hands, palms facing up, on your lap, in a receptive, relaxed manner.

It is recommended that you breathe through your nose during the meditations. If you cannot, it is okay. You may also choose to put the tip of your tongue on the roof of your mouth as you meditate. [pause]

Begin to relax your body. Bring your focus to your breath. Without changing anything or judging anything, just notice your breath—the rise and fall of your breath. Notice your breathing at this moment. Observe your body and your breath. [pause]

Bring your attention to where your body is supported. If you are on a chair, notice where your body touches the chair. Feel your body fully supported. Now bring your attention to your feet and notice where they are resting on the ground.

Continue to quiet yourself by slowing and deepening your breath. Sink into a quiet space within. Feel your breath moving through your body. Tune in to the beating of your heart. Allow yourself to go a little deeper into a quiet space within.

Begin to inhale to the count of three... and exhale a little more slowly to the count of four. [pause]

Use this breathing pattern to transition into a relaxed and receptive mode. This is not a time for analysis. Let any thoughts or concerns that come up in your mind pass by like clouds passing across the sky. [pause]

The next step is to add musical words to the breathing pattern. This is done silently and subtly. Let the words ride on your breath, going in and out.

For a slow count of three... quietly breathe in as you focus on the three syllables "Mu-sic Path."

And then to a slow count of four... breathe out as you focus on the four syllables "Il-lu-mi-nates."

Go a little deeper into the stillness by repeating this mantra, as the words silently ride in and out on your breath. [pause]

You can expand the practice by pausing at the top and the bottom of your breath. Honor the natural rhythm of your body. Allow your breath to ride on the words as you inhale "Music Path" and exhale "Illuminates."

Notice whatever comes to you. Dwell in the quiet space deep within. [pause]

Imagine yourself in a beautiful setting in nature. In front of you is a long path. Far in the distance, you see a figure walking toward you, looking happy to see you. As this figure gets closer, you recognize it is you, as your Future Musical Self, developed by the guidance of your musical muse.

What do you notice about your Future Musical Self? *[pause]*

Stay in the quiet space and be with this experience. Just notice what comes. [pause]

 It is time to journal.

Staying in a light meditative state, pick up your writing method of choice. You will ask your Future Musical Self several questions. Words, images, feelings, sparks, or flashes may bubble up. Sometimes a surprise may come. Feel free to use the pages in the back, or your Companion Journal, for more room. Journal until you fee complete.

Ask with an open heart and journal on these prompts...

What would you like me to know about my musicality? *[pause]*

How can I move forward on my musical path? *[pause]*

What abilities have you developed that were most rewarding and exciting? *[pause]*

What have been the most surprising parts of your musical journey? *[pause]*

What is your primary instrument? *[pause]*

What other instruments do you play? *[pause]*

Is there an instrument you wish you had learned to play? *[pause]*

Do you sing? *[pause]*

What else would you like me to know at this moment? *[pause]*

Soon you will bring your encounter to a close.

Thank your Future Musical Self for coming through in any way it did to be with you today. Feel your heart filled with gratitude. *[pause]*

See your Future Musical Self walk back down the path into the distance until you can no longer see them. Gently deepen your breath. *[pause]*

Take a few more long, slow, deep breaths as you integrate this experience. *[pause]*

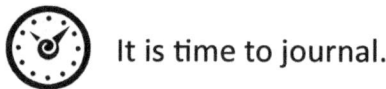 It is time to journal.

There are two steps left.

First, you will journal on your experience of the meditation. Trust any impressions, flashes, words, or anything else that comes.

Journal for five minutes or more, then find a good stopping place. You may begin now.
[long pause to journal]

The final step is to read what you just wrote from a curious and neutral perspective. After you have read your new journal entry, journal on what you notice about it. Feel free to use the pages in the back (Section Three), or your Companion Journal, or another writing medium to respond to the following prompts. Journal until you feel complete.

What occurs to you about your journal entry?

Do you notice any themes or patterns?

Are there any surprises?

Remember, your journaling is for your eyes only, so allow yourself to fully express your deepest desires and curiosities on the page. This final step of reflective journaling is often fruitful and revealing.

Staying in a quiet and receptive space, let it flow through you. It is time to journal again for a final five minutes. You may begin journaling now. *[long pause to journal]*

Is there anything else to record at this moment while it is fresh in your mind?

It is time to bring your writing to a good stopping place for now. This is the end of the Future Musical Self Meditation. You've taken a new step on your Musician's Heart Journey. More insights will likely come to you about this experience. You can return to your journal anytime to explore and develop this work.

Illuminating the Path Forward: Reading, Reviewing, and Reflecting

The last step of this method is where the greatest illuminations often come. Reading your own writing and noticing the insights in your own words is the fruit of this labor. Journal deeply on the last step of this method for a rewarding experience of self-discovery.

It is important to make an internal agreement that you will read, review, and reflect upon your journal entry through a neutral and compassionate lens. Choose to come from an encouraging place that is free from criticism. This is your musical muse expressing itself in a great variety of ways to reveal the many possibilities available to you.

The insights you receive point you in the direction of your heart-centered next step on your musical journey. Any negative self-talk impedes the journey. If you find yourself writing in a critical tone, simply notice it and transmute it at once into a positive voice dedicated to your fulfillment as a being who loves music-making.

Here are two examples:

Remember Robert, the percussionist who loved the idea of playing the cello? In reviewing his journal entry, he wrote:

> *The desire to play the cello comes up again and again in my journaling. There is something there for me. I could research beginner cello lessons. I even have a bunch of older drums I could trade for a cello. I wonder if I could learn to play a song on it by the holidays.*

After reading her entry, Marie, wrote:

> *When I asked my future musical self "Do you sing?" I felt a huge surge of energy inside me. Singing was something I loved to do when I was young. I was in three choruses! I forgot how much I love singing. Actually I sang in a chorus in my young adult life as well. That makes four! The vibration was sublime. When we all harmonized, my eyes would sometimes fill up with tears of sheer joy. There are no words to describe those moments. I wonder if there is an adult choir in my area.*

Provisions for the Journey

A Paradigm Shift

Your time at Base Camp is complete. It is time to pack up for the next leg of the journey. Superfluous material will be left behind. The less you have to carry, the more enjoyable the journey will be.

On this passage of the journey, you will learn how to lighten your metaphorical load. The uncharted territory is a new experience of listening deeply to your inner whispers. Those inklings can be dismissed or overlooked. Often those whispers are the ones that most authentically call you in the direction of your true musical desires.

The superfluous, heavy baggage you are leaving behind is the voices of destruction. These critical narratives replay in your psyche and sabotage your Musician's Heart Journey.

These are the voices of the past and present. In addition to what other people have said to you, there may also be damaging inner attitudes to examine and release.

This is nothing short of a paradigm shift. By tapping into a channel of insight and brilliance found inside, you will navigate your journey in alignment with your true musical nature.

To begin, you will choose your provisions through an inner lens. External musical goals have great value, and they will be explored later in this work. However, at this moment, you will pack your metaphorical backpack with provisions that promote self-reliance, resourcefulness, inner inspiration, and versatility. Once your inner world is aligned with your heart's desire, your outer world will begin to reflect it.

"The sculpture is already complete within the marble block, before I start my work. It is already there, I just have to chisel away the superfluous material."

– MICHELANGELO

Voices Remembered, Voices Released

In this exercise, you will identify the burdensome baggage of the past which could sabotage your journey ahead.

Take on this task knowing that unexpected harmful and damaging memories may reveal themselves.

This exercise can point to clues of what may have stunted your musical growth. Even the slightest perception of judgment can shut down the spirit of a budding musician.

This is meant to be done quickly—think bullet points. This is not the time for detailed journaling. This exercise is intended to create a broad-brush picture of your musical influences.

Flexibility and resourcefulness are imperative for this journey. Honor your intuitions and instincts. Notice everything that shows up, especially what surprises you.

🕐 It is time to journal. Take no more than 1 or 2 minutes on each of the following journal prompts. The objective here is to get a bird's-eye perspective on any significant negative influences, voices, or beliefs in your musical experience. Again, for this part of the journey, be sure to focus on negative influences or memories. They may be buried deep inside, so notice what comes up and list it, no matter how insignificant it might seem at first.

As a child...

As a teenager...

As a young adult...

About my music-making, my Mom said...

My Dad said...

My sister/brother said...

A friend said...

The kids at school said...

My musical director said...

Who else negatively influenced my musical experience?

What other event(s) or experience(s) created a negative experience?

A painful memory of music-making is...

As I remember it...

I believed...

because ...

My biggest struggle, when it comes to moving forward with my musical passion, has been...

Inner Dialogue Check-In. Are these the kind of things you say to yourself?

I made that mistake again. Am I ever going to get it right? I hope nobody can hear me practice. I have no time to practice. What's the point?

How can you best move forward with your musicality despite these painful experiences?

Journaling can liberate and heal you as you reveal your pain on the page. Some memories may require your forgiveness. Why sacrifice your musical dreams based on someone else's opinion?

It is time to release any painful memories or beliefs. There is no room for them among your provisions.

You now stand at a powerful crossroad...

Releasing Meditation at the Crossroad

 The musical breath mantra used for this meditation is "Musical Empowerment." Begin to relax your body and drop down into a quiet space deep inside.

Let these words silently ride on your breath.

Inhale for a slow count of three to the syllables "Mus-i-cal."

Then exhale for a slow count of four to the syllables "Em-pow-er-ment."

Take a few minutes to relax your body and mind. Allow yourself to go a little deeper with each breath. [pause]

Imagine yourself looking directly at an enormous crossroad of two large dirt roads that extend as far as you can see. In the very center of the crossroad is a group of people. These people represent the discouraging voices and moments you just wrote about. They are all talking loudly at the same time. It is a cacophony of unpleasant noise. In your mind's eye, see them as one loud group on the crossroad. [pause]

Imagine you have control of the volume of these voices by turning a holographic knob, like on a stereo. Begin to turn down the knob. Simultaneously, as you turn down the volume, imagine the visual image of the group begins to get smaller and more transparent. Imagine you start to see right through them. [pause]

Continue to turn down the knob. As the volume gets softer, the vision of the group continues to shrink and get even more transparent. Gradually, the sight and sound of them fade out until they are completely gone. [pause]

All that remains is a small mound of dirt on the crossroad. Imagine a strong wind suddenly picks up. A little tornado forms and picks up the mound of dirt, then hurls it powerfully into space dispersing it in a thousand directions. The crossroad is once again quiet and peaceful. The wind returns to a gentle breeze. [pause]

Take a few deep breaths and exhale with an audible sigh.

 It is time to journal about this experience. You may need more time and space than is provided on this next page. You can also use the pages in the back (Section Three).

Musical Library Meditation

This meditation has been recorded by the author and can be downloaded for an audible experience. Go to musiciansheartjourney.com to sign up to receive this free gift as well as other valuable resources.

Come to a seated position with both feet on the ground. Sit with a comfortably straight spine. You can be lying down if necessary, but it may be easy to fall asleep that way. Explore what posture works best for you.

Have this Journal or another writing medium of your choice nearby, but not in your hands or on your body. Put everything else down and place your hands, palms facing up, on your lap, in a receptive, relaxed manner.

It is recommended that you breathe through your nose during the meditations. If you cannot, it is okay. You may also choose to put the tip of your tongue on the roof of your mouth as you meditate. [pause]

Begin to relax your body. Bring your focus to your breath. Without changing anything or judging anything, just notice your breath—the rise and fall of your breath. Notice your breathing at this moment. Observe your body and your breath. [pause]

Bring your attention to where your body is supported. If you are on a chair, notice where your body touches the chair. Feel your body fully supported. Now bring your attention to your feet and notice where they are resting on the ground. Continue to quiet yourself by slowing and deepening your breath. Sink into a quiet space within. Feel your breath moving through your body. Tune in to the beating of your heart.

Allow yourself to go a little deeper into a quiet space within. Begin to inhale to the count of three [pause] and exhale a little more slowly to the count of four. [pause]

Use this breathing pattern to transition into a relaxed and receptive mode. This is not a time for analysis. Let any thoughts or concerns that come up in your mind pass by like clouds passing across the sky. [pause]

The next step is to add musical words to the breathing pattern. This is done silently and subtly. Let the words ride on your breath, going in and out.

For a slow count of three, quietly breathe in as you focus on the three syllables "Lis-ten-ing."

And then to a slow count of four, breathe out as you focus on the four syllables "and Qui-et-ing."

Go a little deeper into the stillness by repeating this mantra, as the words silently ride in and out on your breath. [pause]

You can expand the practice by pausing at the top and the bottom of your breath. Honor the natural rhythm of your body. Allow your breath to ride on the words as you inhale "Listening" and exhale "and Quieting."

Notice whatever comes to you. Dwell in the quiet space deep within. [long pause]

Imagine you are standing in front of a magnificent library. [pause]

See the steps leading up to the library's entrance. Walk up the steps. In front of you is a large, ornate door. Take a moment to notice the door. [pause]

This door is a musical portal. Open the door and walk into the library. As you walk through this portal, you leave behind your current musical ability and enter a place of total musical mastery. In this library, you can play any instrument exquisitely. You have all musical scores internally encoded in your memory and can play anything effortlessly. You have the voice of an angel. Rhythm plays through you in intuitive and complex patterns. Your ability to write music is unbridled and brilliant. You are all-musical. Indeed, you are music embodied, and music expresses itself through you in numerous ways.

Feel into this realm. [pause]

Notice what stirs inside you. [pause]

In front of you is a corridor leading to the center of the library. Begin to walk toward the center of the library.

As you walk, look around and notice what you see. [pause]

In the center of the library, you discover a grand rotunda with a soaring, domed ceiling adorned with glorious artwork and a large skylight at the top.

Take a moment to notice the rotunda's ceiling. [pause]

The library is quiet and peaceful, yet you can feel the subtle vibrations of all music of the past, present, and future. In the library, thousands of instruments are available, all in perfect working order and ready to be played. Here, you have access to all music. You can talk to, or play with, any musician from any era. [pause]

In the center of the rotunda, there is a large circle on the marble floor. On it is a symbol of music. Take a moment to notice the symbol. [pause]

Walk to the center of the circle. Notice the large skylight directly overhead. Light showers through the skylight, brightly illuminating the center of the rotunda and you. Bathe in the sunlight and feel the warm sunbeams enliven your deep connection to music. Allow the light to pour into you until you are full of light. Take a moment to notice how the light feels as it illuminates your body. [pause]

There are numerous corridors extending to other areas of the library. Each one leads to one of many musical worlds you may explore. One corridor leads to a world of rhythm where you can play any percussion instrument with any musician or by yourself. Master musicians are available at all times to play with you or teach you what you would like to learn. Another corridor leads to a world of wind instruments where you can play a flute that is more than 40,000 years old, made of the bone from the neck of a bird.

Imagine all the corridors and possible places that are available for your exploration. [pause]

Which one calls to you now? [pause]

Be open to the encouragement of your musical muse. The sky is the limit on how your musical muse whispers to you. Flashes, images, inklings, feelings, or impressions may come to you. Take a few minutes and choose a corridor to explore the musical world that intrigues you most. [pause]

Take at least five minutes to meditate now. Explore the musical world of your choice. Stay in the quiet and be receptive to what comes. [long pause]

In a minute, you will begin to bring this visit to a close. [pause]

When you are ready, thank any musicians or teachers who have shown up for you. Make your way back up the corridor to the grand rotunda. Take a moment to look around the rotunda and see if there is anything else you notice today. [pause]

At another time, you can come back to explore another corridor representing another musical curiosity that calls to you. The Musical Library is open for you at all times.

When you feel complete, see yourself walking back to the front door of the library. Open it, and walk out. As you walk back down the steps, know that you can return here any time you wish.

Gently deepen your breath. [pause]

Begin to wiggle your toes. Lightly rub your hands together. Perhaps even brush them over your face and back over your head. Take a deep breath and exhale with an audible sigh. Come back fully to the present space and time. [pause]

Give yourself a few minutes to come to closure with this meditation. Continue to take a few more long, slow, deep breaths to help you integrate this experience. [pause]

🕐 It is time to journal on the following prompts.

What was the musical symbol on the floor, and what does it signify to you? *[pause]*

Did you meet with, or play with, any musicians? *[pause]*

What musical abilities did you have in the library? *[pause]*

What corridor did you explore? *[pause]*

musiciansheartjourney.com

What else did you experience in the library? *[pause]*

Were there any surprises? *[pause]*

Is there anything else you want to record from this visit to the library? *[pause]*

Next, you will journal on your overall experience of the meditation. Trust any impressions, flashes, words, or anything else that came to you. Journal for five minutes or more, then find a good stopping place. You can also use the pages in the back or your Companion Journal.
[long pause]

The final step is to read what you just wrote from a curious and neutral perspective. Notice any impressions, flashes, words, or anything else that comes to you. Go ahead now and read your writing then use these prompts to explore and illuminate your experience.

What occurs to you about your journal entry?

Do you notice any themes or patterns?

Are there any surprises?

Remember, your journaling is for your eyes only, so allow yourself to fully express your deepest truths and experiences. This final step of reflective journaling is often most revealing. Staying in a quiet and receptive space, let it flow through you.

Is there anything else to record at this moment while it is fresh in your mind?

It is time to bring your writing to a good stopping place for now.

This is the end of the Musical Library Meditation.

You've taken a new step on your Musician's Heart Journey. More insights will likely come to you about this experience. You can return to your journal anytime to explore and develop this work.

Create Your Musical Timeline

Next, you will create a musical timeline of your joyous musical memories. This process will contribute to your map you will soon create. Use one-liners for responses. If you are new to music-making, you can journal about what has drawn you to music over the years.

Do this exercise quickly. This is not time for luxurious journaling. In each category, list your activity as well as relevant memories. The following timeline examples are provided to help you understand the scope and structure of this process.

Example: Claire

Claire is a middle-aged woman whose children are grown and gone. She used to enjoy playing her guitar. Years ago, she used to play for Hospice as a volunteer, but it has been years since she's been an active and developing musician.

Claire's Musical Timeline

Childhood: Played guitar—took lessons since I was 9. I was the only one in the family to play an instrument.

Middle School: Joined the choir as an alto. Learned to harmonize.

High School: Studied music theory. Music was very important to my identity, more than any other subject. Joined the choir and sang throughout high school years. Loved, loved, LOVED being in the choir.

College: Studied guitar for one year, then transferred to a different college where I stopped studying guitar. I joined the choir which I was in for two years. Did holiday concerts. Traveled to England with the choir and had a blast.

Young Adult: Got married. Tried to play guitar again but had forgotten so much. Bought a classical guitar but felt intimidated. Joined a local choir. Very relaxed atmosphere and nice people. We adored singing together.

Age 30-50: Busy raising children. My daughter played the silver flute so I tried to pick up the guitar again so I could play with her. Couldn't recall enough.

Age 50 and over: Yearning for a musical tribe. It is not the same, just playing by myself. I can't seem to get anywhere on my own. I need a goal or some sort of guidance and support.

Example: Kevin

Kevin is a career mechanic in his 50s. Learning to play a musical instrument just for fun is a new idea for him. Music has always seemed like a foreign language to Kevin. Being a mechanic for decades, he naturally tries to figure out what makes something work and how it ticks. His analytical mind will serve him well on his musical journey.

Kevin's Musical Timeline

Childhood: Took music classes in elementary school. Learned some basics.

Middle School: Tried to play the cello but only lasted one year. I was too shy and I was afraid to play in front of people. I hated to practice but I liked the sound of the cello.

High School: Enjoyed playing the radio in the car with my friends.

College: Nothing I can remember.

Young Adult: Enjoyed listening to church music. I liked the ones that had the instruments from the orchestra.

Age 30-50: Married a music teacher.

Age 50 and over: I'm starting to understand music. Talking with my wife, I mentioned if I could play an instrument, I'd choose the violin. Then she went out and got me one. I always felt that music was too complex to understand. I am starting to understand music as I'm learning to tune my violin. I wonder if I could learn to repair a violin.

"Whether you think you can or you think you can't, you're right."
– HENRY FORD

It is time to journal. Using the space below, make an index about *joyous* musical memories you recall. If music-making is new to you, you can journal about what you enjoyed about music in these stages of your life.

Childhood:

Kindergarten through Middle School:

High School:

College:

Young Adult:

Age 30-50:

Age 50 and over:

When Claire read over her Musical Timeline, she saw that she had forgotten about being in a choir for much of her early life. It was always such a joyous experience for her. How could she have forgotten about all the choirs she had been in? Her own writing revealed this vital pattern to her.

When Kevin read over his list, he realized that music is not all that difficult to understand and that he had an early interest in string instruments. Now he was curious about repairing them. He thought he didn't have much musical experience, but now he saw he had an interest all along.

Look at your list.

Are there any repeated patterns or themes?

What stands out as inspiring or surprising to you?

Make Your Musical Wishlist

With your magic wand in hand, disguised as a writing instrument, list up to 10 top mind-blowing musical desires you can imagine for yourself. The sky is the limit, so think big!

Here are Claire and Kevin's top musical desires:

Claire's List

Learn to play flamenco guitar and play in a local band or for Hospice

Play by ear instead of always using sheet music

Find other people to play with and invite them over

Have a beautiful practice space with lots of instruments for friends to play when visiting

Get excellent instruction from an online teacher

Create a practice schedule I can stick to

Download a tuner app on my phone

Learn about loopers

Record myself singing

Write a song, maybe a duet

Kevin's List

Play the violin well

Be able to hear a note and know what it is

Put a visual guide on my violin and learn the notes

Feel comfortable playing in front of others

Know how to care for my violin

Learn how to change the strings and make adjustments

 It is time to journal. Here you will draft your first list.

Reviewing your list, put a "1" next to the ones that stir something inside you. These choices are fascinating enough that you would like to explore them!

Put a "2" next to the ones that "would be nice" but probably aren't your first choice right now.

Put a "3" next to the goals you want to keep on the radar. These spark some interest, and perhaps in the future you may pursue them, but not right now. *[long pause to review and rank your list]*

If there is more than one #1 choice, consider them, take a few breaths, and quiet yourself.

 It is time to journal and choose the goal you will pursue at this time.

What fills my musician's heart most is...

The musical desire I most want to explore now is...

Congratulations! You have your initial Musician's Heart Journey goal. The last step is to use these insights and everything else you have done thus far on your journey to create a musical vision board. Organic and powerful messages, from deep inside, may reveal your musical heart's desire.

"Do whatever brings you to life. Then follow your own fascinations, obsessions, and compulsions. Trust them. Create whatever causes a revolution in your heart."
– ELIZABETH GILBERT, *BIG MAGIC: CREATIVE LIVING BEYOND FEAR*

Map Your Journey: Create a Musical Vision Board

 It is time to develop your musical vision board. Each one is unique. Through the exercises in this section, your map will begin to appear before your eyes. Allow yourself to take a deep dive into your creativity as you develop this piece of art. Savor the process. There is no rush to get this done. It may take you days or even weeks to complete this. Let the artwork evolve and reveal what is inside of you.

Ideas

Make a life-sized silhouette of yourself on white paper. You can get a large roll of paper or simply take numerous pieces of paper you have on hand, to create a large canvas for yourself. Be sure to leave large margins all around the silhouette. Find an ideal wall area to work on this project. If you are using a big roll of paper, painter's tape, all the way around, and thumbtacks should hold it in place.

Position yourself on the wall and have someone draw your silhouette, taking care to preserve your details. If you'd like to include your instrument, hold your instrument if that is feasible. You could also draw a large instrument over the body's silhouette or inside the body after your silhouette is defined.

Instead of a body silhouette, you could draw your instrument or another instrument that interests you. This is your musical vision board, so make it anything you wish!

Observing the silhouette, let thoughts, images, and impressions come to you. Artwork will soon fill this silhouette, but right now, your musical vision board is open and full of possibility. Fill it with colors, words, shapes, symbols, quotes, authentic yearnings, musical "bucket list" items, and even your greatest musical desire. Make it your own! Let yourself dream while you honor anything you'd like on your musical vision board.

Other ideas:
- Create a mind-map or doodle.
- Draw an instrument and go from there.
- Choose words that come to you.
- Make up your own musical breath mantra and incorporate it into your artwork.
- Think up a new journal prompt and journal on that.
- Trace the outline of your hand on a piece of paper and color it in an inspiring way.

Although this work is highly visual, you are a journaler, after all. You know how writing can often bring clarity. Use words directly on your musical vision board that are powerful for you. Visions may flash in your mind. Anything goes on your vision board! Remember to journal about this process to explore ideas. The following pages are examples.Although this work is highly visual, you are a journaler, after all. You know how writing can often bring clarity. Use words directly on your musical vision board that are powerful for you. Visions may flash in your mind. Anything goes on your vision board! Remember to journal about this process to explore ideas. The following pages are examples.

"You are full of music!"

– MARY KNYSH, INTERNATIONAL TRAINER FOR THE *MUSIC FOR PEOPLE* ORGANIZATION

These creations are thumbnail versions of life-size paintings which started as silhouettes.

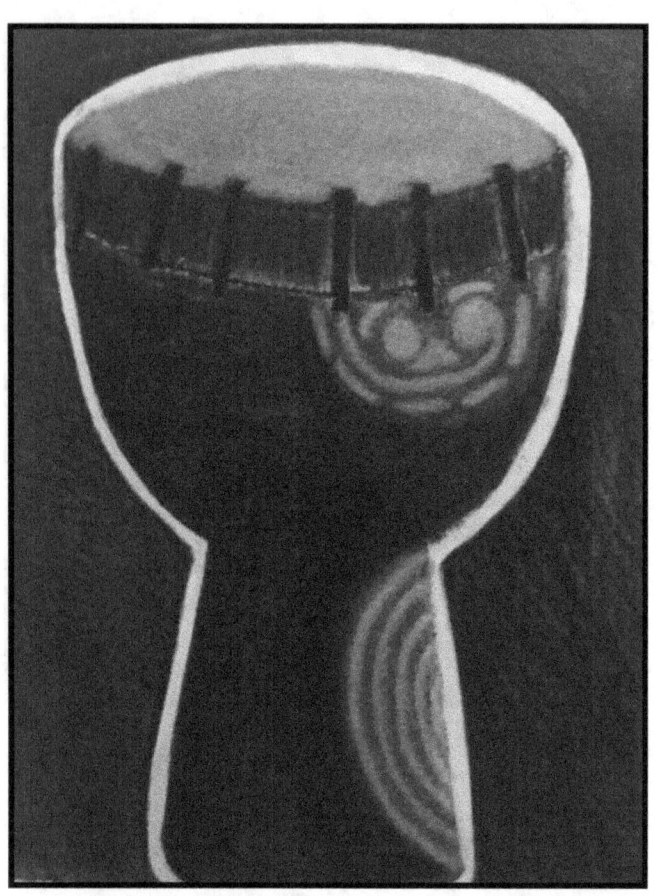
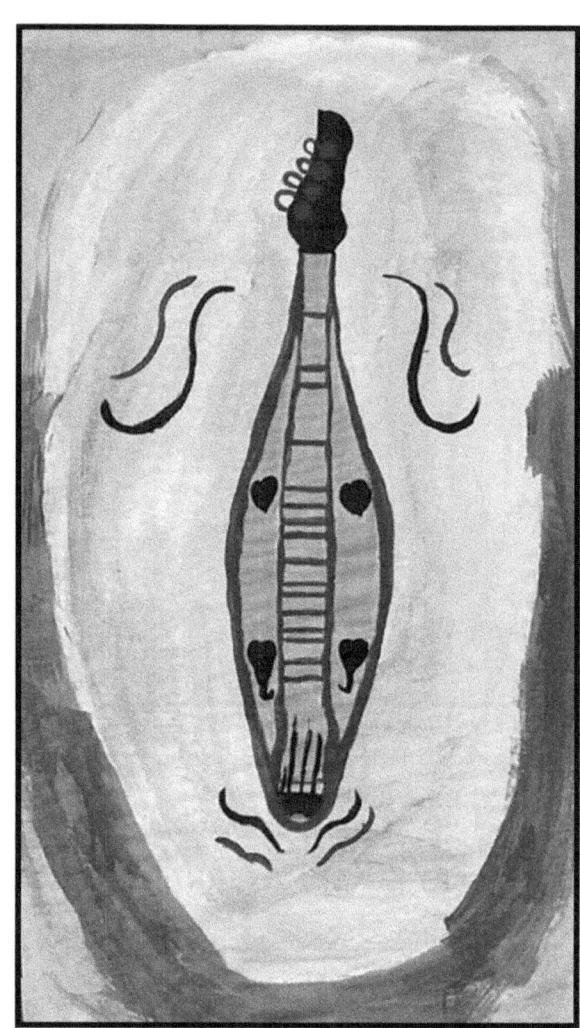

Charcoal black and white art above by Alan Tracy.

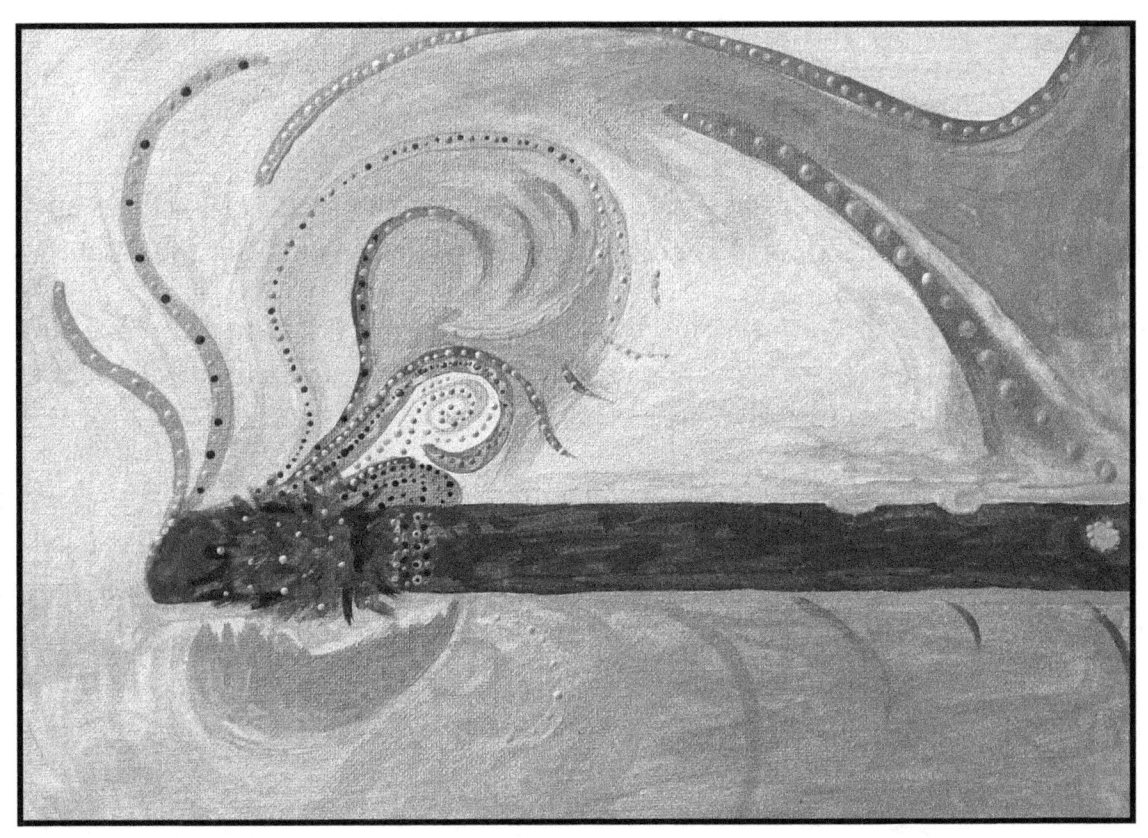

Learn to Use Your Compass

Open up this Journal to the Weekly Daytimer section which starts on page 60 of this book. See the stand-alone *Weekly Daytimers* and *Companion Journals* available in small, medium, and large sizes on musiciansheartjourney.com.

Take your chosen goals, your musical vision board, and all the insights you now have, and get ready to learn how to use the two repeating weekly tools: the Compass (one week's plan) and the Magnifying Glass (weekly written Reflections).

Using these tools, you have a sustainable, self-directed guidance system. Look at the blank left-hand page below. This page is your Compass that keeps you on track. Each week you will use this page to prepare for the next leg of your journey, in one-week segments. Next week, the plan may be different, but for the coming week, you have your direction.

Compass (left page)

> *"If I don't practice for a day, I know it. If I don't practice for two days, the critics know it. And if I don't practice for three days, the public knows it."*
>
> **– LOUIS ARMSTRONG**

Let's compare this approach to driving a car at night. In the dark, your headlights only illuminate the road immediately in front of you. That is all you need to see at that moment. Similarly, your weekly Compass illuminates your musical path immediately in front of you, which is this week.

Can you recall Aesop's fable about the tortoise and the hare? Remember, the slow and steady tortoise wins the race! It is time to start using your Compass by making your weekly plan. Here's where the rubber meets the road. Making your weekly plan using your Compass gives you traction and momentum.

Here is Claire's plan. Structure works well for her, so she proactively segments her days into focused practice themes, as seen below.

Claire's Plan

BIG VISION: play Flamenco guitar for fun, soloing, and playing confidently with others

Monday - Arpeggios

Tuesday - Chord progressions

Wednesday - Alexander Technique every other week, online lesson every other week

Thursday - Familiar repertoire

Friday - Improvise with friends

Saturday - New repertoire

Sunday - Explore YouTube for inspiration

With her weekly Compass set, Claire is no longer confused or overwhelmed with her musical goals. What happens when you don't get to your practice on a particular day? We all know that life *happens*, so when your plans get derailed, simply choose to continue moving forward in the direction of your musical goals the next day. The journey is productive as long as you are consistent with and focused on your practice. Get creative on how and where to practice. Try getting out of your comfort zone by bringing your instrument to work and light up your workplace! You never know who you will inspire! Be resourceful and flexible.

Schedule Your Practice

Your music-making is a joyous and vital part of your life and identity. Set your intention for your progress. Consider segmenting your practice. Start by answering these questions.

 It is time to journal. Respond to these questions to formulate a practice routine that works best for your life.

What time of day are my physical energy and mental focus the best?

When will I most likely not get interrupted?

Do I want to practice with others?

If I play with others, how can I still find time to practice on my own?

How can I practice most effectively?

Am I willing to put everything else on hold for at least 10 minutes a day for focused practice?

When setting up my Compass, have I considered what else is happening this week in my household?

By sticking to your plan, you show up for *yourself* just like you would show up at any other appointment on your calendar. Declare your BIG VISION, if you wish, by writing it on the top of the Compass (left-hand page of Weekly Daytimer). Set a goal for the week and keep that goal in mind, allowing it to be the guiding light that moves you forward on your journey.

Always be gentle with yourself on the journey and remember that the tortoise wins the race. Be the tortoise—steadfast, relentless, and committed. Make progress every day.

10-minute Daily Practice Shots Keep You Moving Forward Musically

Even 10 minutes a day will keep you connected to your goal and going in the right direction. If you can practice more, that is better. Commit to a minimum of 10 minutes of focused and intentional practice daily. Be sure to record it on the Compass page.

That 10 minutes might (and hopefully will) lead to another 10-minute practice that day, and maybe more. Even if you only practice for 10 minutes a day, your consistent effort yields real progress and keeps you in the game when you don't think you have time for practice.

Here is what your 10-minute daily practice shots yield over the course of a year:

If you practice just 10 minutes a day, you will have played your instrument a respectable 60 hours in one year.

Two daily 10-minute practices will yield just over 120 hours.

Three daily 10-minute practices will yield a solid 180 hours for the year.

It is recommended that you record the beginning and ending time on your Compass page. This habit makes you aware of how much time you are putting into your musical pursuits.

It is time to make your first weekly plan. As you set up your first weekly Compass, consider the following: your instrument, the music you are learning, and if you are preparing for a future event like a holiday concert or a gig. Do your best to consider your instrument, where you are going, and how to acquire the necessary skills to make progress with your musicality.

For example, if you are learning to play guitar, practice topics could be:

- Work on a new scale
- Work on a new finger pattern
- Listen deeply, with no distractions, to a recording of a musician who inspires you
- Learn a new rhythm
- Work on familiar repertoire
- Learn one new song
- Improvise in a new key
- Dexterity practice
- Research new material
- Solo playing
- Group playing
- Get private lessons to accelerate your musical learning in person or online

If you are learning to play a wind instrument or working with your voice or didgeridoo, you would likely include breath control exercises.

These ideas are just the beginning of the possibilities!

Consider the week ahead and arrange your focused practice themes on the days that make the most sense. You can revise your plan next week. This week's Compass points you in the direction you have declared.

"What the mind can conceive, the mind can achieve."

— NAPOLEON HILL

It is time to create your first weekly Compass. This process will get easier each week. Use this as a starting point. Consider your possible focused practice themes and schedule them.

Monday

Tuesday

Wednesday

Thursday

Friday

Saturday

Sunday

Keep the commitment of at least 10 minutes a day and track it in on your Compass. The mere act of writing something down every single day on your Compass keeps you connected and moving forward on your Musician's Heart Journey. Go for three shots of 10 minutes whenever possible.

See Claire's Compass on the following page. See how she logs her musical pursuits.

Claire's Compass (left page)

Monday *Arpeggios*   7:25pm-8:10pm   45 min
Use Andalusian Cadence, A,G,F,E
Metronome 63,65,67 bpm
Good practice tonight, left hand is getting stronger.

Tuesday *Chord progressions*
7am-7:15am 4-3-2-1 starting at A   15 min
4:30pm-4:45pm 4-3-2-1 starting at C   15 min

Wednesday *Alexander Technique*   7pm-8:30pm   90 min

Thursday *Familiar songs*   7:45pm-9:15pm   90 min
Family jam session in living room. This is what it is all about :)
New interest in the family with the violin, tiny instrument, big voice.

Friday *Improvisation*   6:30pm-8:15pm   105 min
Friends over, playing all kinds of stuff, new blues tune
Feeling more confident with solos

Saturday *New songs*   11:30am-12:15pm   45 min
New download Edelweiss
Reflections journaling

Sunday *Listening, exploring YouTube*   8:45pm-9:30pm   45 min
Percussive guitar, new styles emerging
Will try next week at family jam

Learn to Use Your Magnifying Glass

The Magnifying Glass will inform your plan for the week ahead. Below is an example of the Magnifying Glass, which is the right-hand side of the Weekly Daytimer. These Reflection questions are meant to be done consistently and with great intrigue. Try to do them on a consistent day each week to set yourself up for success. Consider your coming week, pick a day that works best, and schedule it on your Compass for the following week.

Magnifying Glass (right page)

This Week's Reflections

What was a musical highlight for me this week?

What inspirations emerged from it?

This week, I listened to

In the coming week...

My musical musings could be

The one that excites me the most is

To make this happen, I will say NO to

...and I will say YES to

I will stretch my musical comfort zone this week by

By aligning with your inner musical truth each week, you enter into a relationship with your music with momentum and meaning. In this process of deep reflection, wonderment, and honesty, you may find valuable insights into your effort of the past week. It will also set you up nicely by informing the next step on your journey.

Robin

Robin, a 34-year old Frenchwoman living her dream in London, makes her living as a photo-journalist for a travel magazine. Growing up, she played clarinet in the band at school. She took to the harmonica since it fit in so well with her tiny-carbon-footprint lifestyle, and she became brilliantly skilled at it. Harmonica is her new instrument.

She writes, *"People still ask me sometimes if a harmonica is considered a real instrument. Then I blow them away with a tune or two. I like watching their faces as they hear me play!"*

Since you have not logged a week's worth of practice yet on your Compass page, go ahead read through the intentional questions and prompts to familiarize yourself with them.

"It's not the destination, it's the journey."

— RALPH WALDO EMERSON

Robin's Magnifying Glass (right page)

This Week's Reflections

What was a musical highlight for me this week? *I came across a DVD series at the library on the origins of country music in America. The story of DeFord Bailey totally floored me. I had heard of him before, but never really checked him out. My honey really enjoyed watching it with me, too. I love these stories about musicians I am finding at the library, and they're FREE!*

What inspirations emerged from it? *Bailey made his harmonica sound like a train. A train! A vehicle, not even a voice or an instrument. This opens up a whole new world for me. What I hear in my everyday life are possible sounds to try. OMG!!*

This week, I listened to *DeFord Bailey YouTube videos. I watched the documentary too.*

In the coming week...

My musical musings could be *Taking a walk around the city during rush hour to listen to traffic sounds for inspiration. I might look at different harmonicas online.*

The one that excites me the most is *Taking a walk around the city for new sound ideas.*

To make this happen, I will say NO to *Spending excessive time on social media.*

...and I will say YES to *I checked the weather forecast. Tues and Wed will be my days for a walk.*

I will stretch my musical comfort zone this week by *Record my favorite city sounds and mix them in with my music.*

As you glance back at your Musician's Heart Journey, acknowledge and celebrate yourself for your openness and sincere efforts!

You have learned to:

- ♫ use the Musical Breath Meditation to go into the quiet.
- ♫ visualize and dialogue with your Future Musical Self.
- ♫ identify destructive memories and voices from your past and acquired a tool to release them.
- ♫ choose the provisions for your journey.
- ♫ make your Musical Timeline and examine it for patterns and insights.
- ♫ create an index of musical goals and choose a starting goal.
- ♫ enter the Musical Library through your mind's eye.
- ♫ give yourself permission to listen deeply to the voice of your inner musical muse.
- ♫ create your Musicial Vision Board to reveal your musical interests.
- ♫ use the Compass (left page of Weekly Daytimer) to navigate practice topics.
- ♫ use the Magnifying Glass (right page of Weekly Daytimer) to gain insight into your experiences from the week.
- ♫ use the pages in the back, or your Companion Journal, for more extensive exploration.
- ♫ journal until you feel complete.

The Open Pages

The last tool of this method is the two Open Pages, which is built in to the Musician's Heart Journey Weekly Daytimers. If you are using something else, simply place two blank pages between your weekly pages to give yourself an open spread of paper following each week. If you are using a notebook or an electronic device, get creative with a reminder to yourself to encourage explorative journaling.

The Open Pages are not to be underestimated. It is here where your inner musical muse loves to dwell. You are learning many new tools to illuminate your path. While the Compass and Magnifying Glass pages provide structure and planning, the Open Pages provide space to further develop insights and a convenient place to jot down ideas that come up throughout the week.

On the Open Pages, your journaling and musical passion have free rein. Let your hand glide around these pages artistically and playfully. Your inklings and curiosities can provide direction for the next leg of your journey.

How to Use the Open Pages Each Week

Right after you have read over your freshly written responses on your Magnifying Glass each week, take notice of what stands out. Look for any patterns. Here you can sink into one of your favorite acts of life: journaling. On the Open Pages, you gain greater insight as you journal, doodle, write music or lyrics, channel a poem, and explore in any way you wish. The Open Pages are your invitation to your musical muse to sing you a song and infuse the coming week.

The following pages offer the stories of Charles and Josie.

Charles

Charles, "Chip" to his wife and close friends, plays the clarinet for a local symphony. The monthly gatherings with his fellow musicians provide him with a sense of identity and rhythm.

Chip has suffered from depression since he was a teenager. He knows in his bones that his music-making and daily journaling have provided the relief and direction he needs to keep him going even through his tough days. He loves to journal and knows how much journaling has helped him sort through his feelings for as long as he can remember. He delights in the simple and earnest act of journaling longhand with a special writing instrument.

When Chip was a teenager, his mother noticed that he loved to journal. On his dark days, he would disappear into his bedroom and journal for hours. For his sixteenth birthday, she gave him a handsome journal with a tiny lock and key, an old-fashioned writing quill, and a box of ink. He treasured her gift and used it through thick and thin, remembering his mother's quiet support and understanding of his struggle.

By using his quill and ink to journal, Chip felt connected with famous writers and composers of the distant past. It became a ritual of self-care for him and a link to the genius that comes through him when he writes. His mother's thoughtfulness cast a loving hue on his chosen coping mechanism of long-hand journaling.

May your journaling in this course bring you comfort and inspiration as it did for Chip. Create a special ritual for your musical adventure so that it a source of continuous growth and delight.

This journaling course concludes with the story of an older lady who found her way back to her joy of music-making, despite her physical limitations.

Josie

Josie is 74 years old. Decades ago, she played the guitar, finger-picking style, with precision and fire. About ten years ago, advanced arthritis developed in her hands and spine making it impossible to play as she did for so many years.

She was always intrigued with the mountain dulcimer, so she decided to take it up. With a little help of a slide, essential oils to relieve her arthritis, and a supportive chair, she became masterful at her new instrument. She took her finger-picking guitar repertoire and salvaged much of it, adapting it to her mountain dulcimer.

Josie loved the look of her mountain dulcimer, which had an unusual body style. It reminded her of a boat. Drawing and painting her new instrument delighted her. She framed it and put it on the wall among her musical instruments and other artwork.

Josie could play her mountain dulcimer on her lap with relative comfort. She felt connected to the players of the past in the mountain towns, out on the porch in the evening, with nothing more than a couple of folk instruments to their names, but with plenty of heart and desire to make music. She found a new friend as she transitioned from playing intricate arrangements on her guitar to more simple music.

"Tell me, what is it you plan to do with your
one wild and precious life?"

– MARY OLIVER

You Are on Your Way!

This journey was created for your private exploration and unique discovery of your true musical passion. For those who love to journal and make music, this method invites you to embrace your adventuresome musical spirit. It also offers a structure to move forward each week toward the goal you hold in your heart for your music-making.

Allow your fearless expression on these pages illuminate the path of your Musician's Heart Journey. May the voice of your inner musical muse be heard, honored, and developed.

If you have gotten insight

and value from this journaling course, please submit a favorable review online.

Great reviews are the lifeblood of an author's career.

Your review is greatly appreciated! Thank you for engaging in this work.

May the voice of your inner musical muse be a source of guidance for your authentic expression on your Musician's Heart Journey.

From my musician's heart to yours,

Ami Sarasvati

"It don't mean a thing, if it ain't got that swing." – Duke Ellington

Monday

Tuesday

Wednesday

Thursday

Friday

Saturday

Sunday

This Week's Reflections

What was a musical highlight for me this week?

What inspirations emerged from it?

This week, I listened to

In the coming week...

My musical musings could be

The one that excites me the most is

To make this happen, I will say NO to

...and I will say YES to

I will stretch my musical comfort zone this week by

"Without music, there is no joy. Without joy, there is no music." – Malinke Proverb

Monday

Tuesday

Wednesday

Thursday

Friday

Saturday

Sunday

This Week's Reflections

What was a musical highlight for me this week?

What inspirations emerged from it?

This week, I listened to

In the coming week...

My musical musings could be

The one that excites me the most is

To make this happen, I will say NO to

...and I will say YES to

I will stretch my musical comfort zone this week by

musiciansheartjourney.com

 *"A simple block of wood, dead by world standards, with hewn love, is given a new body, with breath is giving new life."* – Michael Fuger, Native American Style Flutemaker

Monday

Tuesday

Wednesday

Thursday

Friday

Saturday

Sunday

This Week's Reflections

What was a musical highlight for me this week?

What inspirations emerged from it?

This week, I listened to

In the coming week...

My musical musings could be

The one that excites me the most is

To make this happen, I will say NO to

...and I will say YES to

I will stretch my musical comfort zone this week by

musiciansheartjourney.com

"In my music, I'm trying to play the truth of what I am. The reason it's difficult is because I'm changing all the time." – Charles Mingus

Monday

Tuesday

Wednesday

Thursday

Friday

Saturday

Sunday

This Week's Reflections

What was a musical highlight for me this week?

What inspirations emerged from it?

This week, I listened to

In the coming week...

My musical musings could be

The one that excites me the most is

To make this happen, I will say NO to

...and I will say YES to

I will stretch my musical comfort zone this week by

"In order to understand the music, you need to learn to use your two most important instruments—your left ear and your right." – Doug Kane

Monday

Tuesday

Wednesday

Thursday

Friday

Saturday

Sunday

 *This Week's Reflections*

What was a musical highlight for me this week?

What inspirations emerged from it?

This week, I listened to

In the coming week...

My musical musings could be

The one that excites me the most is

To make this happen, I will say NO to

...and I will say YES to

I will stretch my musical comfort zone this week by

"When you play music you discover a part of yourself that you never knew existed." – Bill Evans

Monday

Tuesday

Wednesday

Thursday

Friday

Saturday

Sunday

This Week's Reflections

What was a musical highlight for me this week?

What inspirations emerged from it?

This week, I listened to

In the coming week...

My musical musings could be

The one that excites me the most is

To make this happen, I will say NO to

...and I will say YES to

I will stretch my musical comfort zone this week by

musiciansheartjourney.com

"Your inner calm is the source of the beauty in the music." – Bernd Geh

Monday

Tuesday

Wednesday

Thursday

Friday

Saturday

Sunday

This Week's Reflections

What was a musical highlight for me this week?

What inspirations emerged from it?

This week, I listened to

In the coming week...

My musical musings could be

The one that excites me the most is

To make this happen, I will say NO to

...and I will say YES to

I will stretch my musical comfort zone this week by

"The truest expression of a people is in its dances and its music. Bodies never lie." – Agnes de Mille

Monday

Tuesday

Wednesday

Thursday

Friday

Saturday

Sunday

This Week's Reflections

What was a musical highlight for me this week?

What inspirations emerged from it?

This week, I listened to

In the coming week...

My musical musings could be

The one that excites me the most is

To make this happen, I will say NO to

...and I will say YES to

I will stretch my musical comfort zone this week by

 *"I want every girl in the world to pick up a guitar and start screaming."* – Courtney Love

Monday

Tuesday

Wednesday

Thursday

Friday

Saturday

Sunday

This Week's Reflections

What was a musical highlight for me this week?

What inspirations emerged from it?

This week, I listened to

In the coming week...

My musical musings could be

The one that excites me the most is

To make this happen, I will say NO to

...and I will say YES to

I will stretch my musical comfort zone this week by

"What makes my approach special is that I do different things. I do jazz, blues, country music and so forth. I do them all, like a good utility man." – Ray Charles

Monday

Tuesday

Wednesday

Thursday

Friday

Saturday

Sunday

This Week's Reflections

What was a musical highlight for me this week?

What inspirations emerged from it?

This week, I listened to

In the coming week...

My musical musings could be

The one that excites me the most is

To make this happen, I will say NO to

...and I will say YES to

I will stretch my musical comfort zone this week by

"I can't stand to sing the same song the same way two nights in succession. If you can, then it ain't music, it's close order drill, or exercise or yodeling or something, not music." – Billie Holiday

Monday

Tuesday

Wednesday

Thursday

Friday

Saturday

Sunday

 # This Week's Reflections

What was a musical highlight for me this week?

What inspirations emerged from it?

This week, I listened to

In the coming week...

My musical musings could be

The one that excites me the most is

To make this happen, I will say NO to

...and I will say YES to

I will stretch my musical comfort zone this week by

"It's very difficult for me to dislike an artist. No matter what he's creating, the fact that he's experiencing the joy of creation makes me feel like we're in a brotherhood of some kind. We're in it together." – Chick Corea

Monday

Tuesday

Wednesday

Thursday

Friday

Saturday

Sunday

This Week's Reflections

What was a musical highlight for me this week?

What inspirations emerged from it?

This week, I listened to

In the coming week...

My musical musings could be

The one that excites me the most is

To make this happen, I will say NO to

...and I will say YES to

I will stretch my musical comfort zone this week by

"Music can change the world." – Ludwig van Beethoven

Monday

Tuesday

Wednesday

Thursday

Friday

Saturday

Sunday

This Week's Reflections

What was a musical highlight for me this week?

What inspirations emerged from it?

This week, I listened to

In the coming week...

My musical musings could be

The one that excites me the most is

To make this happen, I will say NO to

...and I will say YES to

I will stretch my musical comfort zone this week by

"Where words fail, music speaks." – Hans Christian Anderson

Monday

Tuesday

Wednesday

Thursday

Friday

Saturday

Sunday

# This Week's Reflections

What was a musical highlight for me this week?

What inspirations emerged from it?

This week, I listened to

In the coming week...

My musical musings could be

The one that excites me the most is

To make this happen, I will say NO to

...and I will say YES to

I will stretch my musical comfort zone this week by

"Music will be the medicine of the 21st Century!" – *Edgar Cayce*

Monday

Tuesday

Wednesday

Thursday

Friday

Saturday

Sunday

This Week's Reflections

What was a musical highlight for me this week?

What inspirations emerged from it?

This week, I listened to

In the coming week...

My musical musings could be

The one that excites me the most is

To make this happen, I will say NO to

...and I will say YES to

I will stretch my musical comfort zone this week by

"You are responsible for what you think about as you make music. There are the divine moments when the music draws you after itself, and you simply follow." – Stephanie Judy, Making Music for the Joy of It

Monday

Tuesday

Wednesday

Thursday

Friday

Saturday

Sunday

This Week's Reflections

What was a musical highlight for me this week?

What inspirations emerged from it?

This week, I listened to

In the coming week...

My musical musings could be

The one that excites me the most is

To make this happen, I will say NO to

...and I will say YES to

I will stretch my musical comfort zone this week by

 *"The music is not in the notes, but in the silence in between."* – Wolfgang Amadeus Mozart

Monday

Tuesday

Wednesday

Thursday

Friday

Saturday

Sunday

This Week's Reflections

What was a musical highlight for me this week?

What inspirations emerged from it?

This week, I listened to

In the coming week...

My musical musings could be

The one that excites me the most is

To make this happen, I will say NO to

...and I will say YES to

I will stretch my musical comfort zone this week by

"Music is the principle that unites the body, soul, and spirit." – Boethius

Monday

Tuesday

Wednesday

Thursday

Friday

Saturday

Sunday

 This Week's Reflections

What was a musical highlight for me this week?

What inspirations emerged from it?

This week, I listened to

In the coming week...

My musical musings could be

The one that excites me the most is

To make this happen, I will say NO to

...and I will say YES to

I will stretch my musical comfort zone this week by

"You can practice to learn a technique, but I'm more interested in conceiving of something in the moment." – Herbie Hancock

Monday

Tuesday

Wednesday

Thursday

Friday

Saturday

Sunday

This Week's Reflections

What was a musical highlight for me this week?

What inspirations emerged from it?

This week, I listened to

In the coming week...

My musical musings could be

The one that excites me the most is

To make this happen, I will say NO to

...and I will say YES to

I will stretch my musical comfort zone this week by

"Music gives a soul to the universe, wings to the mind, flight to the imagination, and life to everything." – Plato

Monday

Tuesday

Wednesday

Thursday

Friday

Saturday

Sunday

# This Week's Reflections

What was a musical highlight for me this week?

What inspirations emerged from it?

This week, I listened to

In the coming week...

My musical musings could be

The one that excites me the most is

To make this happen, I will say NO to

...and I will say YES to

I will stretch my musical comfort zone this week by

"Where words leave off, music begins." – Heinrich Heine

Monday

Tuesday

Wednesday

Thursday

Friday

Saturday

Sunday

 # This Week's Reflections

What was a musical highlight for me this week?

What inspirations emerged from it?

This week, I listened to

In the coming week...

My musical musings could be

The one that excites me the most is

To make this happen, I will say NO to

...and I will say YES to

I will stretch my musical comfort zone this week by

musiciansheartjourney.com

"Music improvisation is human process in sound. I believe that making music in this way promotes unlimited human potential and joy!" – Mary Knysh

Monday

Tuesday

Wednesday

Thursday

Friday

Saturday

Sunday

This Week's Reflections

What was a musical highlight for me this week?

What inspirations emerged from it?

This week, I listened to

In the coming week...

My musical musings could be

The one that excites me the most is

To make this happen, I will say NO to

...and I will say YES to

I will stretch my musical comfort zone this week by

"I don't sing because I'm happy; I'm happy because I sing." – William James

Monday

Tuesday

Wednesday

Thursday

Friday

Saturday

Sunday

This Week's Reflections

What was a musical highlight for me this week?

What inspirations emerged from it?

This week, I listened to

In the coming week...

My musical musings could be

The one that excites me the most is

To make this happen, I will say NO to

...and I will say YES to

I will stretch my musical comfort zone this week by

 *"Music produces a kind of pleasure which human nature cannot do without."* – *Confucius*

Monday

Tuesday

Wednesday

Thursday

Friday

Saturday

Sunday

This Week's Reflections

What was a musical highlight for me this week?

What inspirations emerged from it?

This week, I listened to

In the coming week...

My musical musings could be

The one that excites me the most is

To make this happen, I will say NO to

...and I will say YES to

I will stretch my musical comfort zone this week by

"You only get better by playing." – Buddy Rich

Monday

Tuesday

Wednesday

Thursday

Friday

Saturday

Sunday

This Week's Reflections

What was a musical highlight for me this week?

What inspirations emerged from it?

This week, I listened to

In the coming week...

My musical musings could be

The one that excites me the most is

To make this happen, I will say NO to

...and I will say YES to

I will stretch my musical comfort zone this week by

"I haven't understood a bar of music in my life, but I have felt it." – Igor Stravinsky

Monday

Tuesday

Wednesday

Thursday

Friday

Saturday

Sunday

This Week's Reflections

What was a musical highlight for me this week?

What inspirations emerged from it?

This week, I listened to

In the coming week...

My musical musings could be

The one that excites me the most is

To make this happen, I will say NO to

...and I will say YES to

I will stretch my musical comfort zone this week by

 *"Music is that which arises in you when reminded by the instruments."* – Walt Whitman

Monday

Tuesday

Wednesday

Thursday

Friday

Saturday

Sunday

This Week's Reflections

What was a musical highlight for me this week?

What inspirations emerged from it?

This week, I listened to

In the coming week...

My musical musings could be

The one that excites me the most is

To make this happen, I will say NO to

...and I will say YES to

I will stretch my musical comfort zone this week by

"When you hear music, after it's over, it's gone in the air. You can never capture it again." – Eric Dolphy

Monday

Tuesday

Wednesday

Thursday

Friday

Saturday

Sunday

This Week's Reflections

What was a musical highlight for me this week?

What inspirations emerged from it?

This week, I listened to

In the coming week...

My musical musings could be

The one that excites me the most is

To make this happen, I will say NO to

...and I will say YES to

I will stretch my musical comfort zone this week by

"For us as a family music is like food; we need it every day; it is basic to life." – Ali Akbar Khan

Monday

Tuesday

Wednesday

Thursday

Friday

Saturday

Sunday

This Week's Reflections

What was a musical highlight for me this week?

What inspirations emerged from it?

This week, I listened to

In the coming week...

My musical musings could be

The one that excites me the most is

To make this happen, I will say NO to

...and I will say YES to

I will stretch my musical comfort zone this week by

"Music is the only source of energy that I have known in my life that gives humans a chance to be instantly transformed into spirit." – David Darling, Music for People Co-Founder

Monday

Tuesday

Wednesday

Thursday

Friday

Saturday

Sunday

# This Week's Reflections

What was a musical highlight for me this week?

What inspirations emerged from it?

This week, I listened to

In the coming week...

My musical musings could be

The one that excites me the most is

To make this happen, I will say NO to

...and I will say YES to

I will stretch my musical comfort zone this week by

"One good thing about music, when it hits you, you feel no pain." – Bob Marley

Monday

Tuesday

Wednesday

Thursday

Friday

Saturday

Sunday

This Week's Reflections

What was a musical highlight for me this week?

What inspirations emerged from it?

This week, I listened to

In the coming week...

My musical musings could be

The one that excites me the most is

To make this happen, I will say NO to

...and I will say YES to

I will stretch my musical comfort zone this week by

"Music is life. Life is Music." – Anonymous

Monday

Tuesday

Wednesday

Thursday

Friday

Saturday

Sunday

This Week's Reflections

What was a musical highlight for me this week?

What inspirations emerged from it?

This week, I listened to

In the coming week...

My musical musings could be

The one that excites me the most is

To make this happen, I will say NO to

...and I will say YES to

I will stretch my musical comfort zone this week by

"My idea is that there is music in the air, music all around us; the world is full of it, and you simply take as much as you require." – Edward Elgar

Monday

Tuesday

Wednesday

Thursday

Friday

Saturday

Sunday

This Week's Reflections

What was a musical highlight for me this week?

What inspirations emerged from it?

This week, I listened to

In the coming week...

My musical musings could be

The one that excites me the most is

To make this happen, I will say NO to

...and I will say YES to

I will stretch my musical comfort zone this week by

"You may say I'm a dreamer, but I'm not the only one. I hope someday you'll join us. And the world will live as one." – John Lennon

Monday

Tuesday

Wednesday

Thursday

Friday

Saturday

Sunday

# This Week's Reflections

What was a musical highlight for me this week?

What inspirations emerged from it?

This week, I listened to

In the coming week...

My musical musings could be

The one that excites me the most is

To make this happen, I will say NO to

...and I will say YES to

I will stretch my musical comfort zone this week by

 *"Music is the strongest form of magic."* – Marilyn Manson

Monday

Tuesday

Wednesday

Thursday

Friday

Saturday

Sunday

This Week's Reflections

What was a musical highlight for me this week?

What inspirations emerged from it?

This week, I listened to

In the coming week...

My musical musings could be

The one that excites me the most is

To make this happen, I will say NO to

...and I will say YES to

I will stretch my musical comfort zone this week by

"You know what music is? It is God's little reminder that there's something else besides us in this universe." – Robin Williams

Monday

Tuesday

Wednesday

Thursday

Friday

Saturday

Sunday

This Week's Reflections

What was a musical highlight for me this week?

What inspirations emerged from it?

This week, I listened to

In the coming week...

My musical musings could be

The one that excites me the most is

To make this happen, I will say NO to

...and I will say YES to

I will stretch my musical comfort zone this week by

"If you wait for tomorrow to follow your dreams, by the time you get there they're gone." – Willie Nelson

Monday

Tuesday

Wednesday

Thursday

Friday

Saturday

Sunday

This Week's Reflections

What was a musical highlight for me this week?

What inspirations emerged from it?

This week, I listened to

In the coming week...

My musical musings could be

The one that excites me the most is

To make this happen, I will say NO to

...and I will say YES to

I will stretch my musical comfort zone this week by

"I am a song, I live to be sung, I sing with all my heart!" – John Denver

Monday

Tuesday

Wednesday

Thursday

Friday

Saturday

Sunday

 # This Week's Reflections

What was a musical highlight for me this week?

What inspirations emerged from it?

This week, I listened to

In the coming week...

My musical musings could be

The one that excites me the most is

To make this happen, I will say NO to

...and I will say YES to

I will stretch my musical comfort zone this week by

"I don't know anything about music, in my line you don't have to." – Elvis Presley

Monday

Tuesday

Wednesday

Thursday

Friday

Saturday

Sunday

This Week's Reflections

What was a musical highlight for me this week?

What inspirations emerged from it?

This week, I listened to

In the coming week...

My musical musings could be

The one that excites me the most is

To make this happen, I will say NO to

...and I will say YES to

I will stretch my musical comfort zone this week by

"In every way, music is our bond between the material and the eternal." – Kenny Werner, Effortless Mastery

Monday

Tuesday

Wednesday

Thursday

Friday

Saturday

Sunday

This Week's Reflections

What was a musical highlight for me this week?

What inspirations emerged from it?

This week, I listened to

In the coming week...

My musical musings could be

The one that excites me the most is

To make this happen, I will say NO to

...and I will say YES to

I will stretch my musical comfort zone this week by

"Music is what feelings sound like." – Anonymous

Monday

Tuesday

Wednesday

Thursday

Friday

Saturday

Sunday

 # This Week's Reflections

What was a musical highlight for me this week?

What inspirations emerged from it?

This week, I listened to

In the coming week...

My musical musings could be

The one that excites me the most is

To make this happen, I will say NO to

...and I will say YES to

I will stretch my musical comfort zone this week by

"Music is the soundtrack to your life." – Dick Clark

Monday

Tuesday

Wednesday

Thursday

Friday

Saturday

Sunday

This Week's Reflections

What was a musical highlight for me this week?

What inspirations emerged from it?

This week, I listened to

In the coming week...

My musical musings could be

The one that excites me the most is

To make this happen, I will say NO to

...and I will say YES to

I will stretch my musical comfort zone this week by

"Music washes away from the soul the dust of everyday life." – Berthold Auerbach

Monday

Tuesday

Wednesday

Thursday

Friday

Saturday

Sunday

This Week's Reflections

What was a musical highlight for me this week?

What inspirations emerged from it?

This week, I listened to

In the coming week...

My musical musings could be

The one that excites me the most is

To make this happen, I will say NO to

...and I will say YES to

I will stretch my musical comfort zone this week by

musiciansheartjourney.com

"You have to take a deep breath and allow the music to flow through you. Revel in it, allow yourself to awe. When you play, allow the music to break your heart with its beauty." – Kelly White

Monday

Tuesday

Wednesday

Thursday

Friday

Saturday

Sunday

This Week's Reflections

What was a musical highlight for me this week?

What inspirations emerged from it?

This week, I listened to

In the coming week...

My musical musings could be

The one that excites me the most is

To make this happen, I will say NO to

...and I will say YES to

I will stretch my musical comfort zone this week by

musiciansheartjourney.com

"When I hear music, I fear no danger. I am invulnerable. I see no foe. I am related to the earliest of times, and to the latest." – Henry David Thoreau

Monday

Tuesday

Wednesday

Thursday

Friday

Saturday

Sunday

This Week's Reflections

What was a musical highlight for me this week?

What inspirations emerged from it?

This week, I listened to

In the coming week...

My musical musings could be

The one that excites me the most is

To make this happen, I will say NO to

...and I will say YES to

I will stretch my musical comfort zone this week by

"Music in the soul can be heard by the universe." – Lao Tzu

Monday

Tuesday

Wednesday

Thursday

Friday

Saturday

Sunday

 *This Week's Reflections*

What was a musical highlight for me this week?

What inspirations emerged from it?

This week, I listened to

In the coming week...

My musical musings could be

The one that excites me the most is

To make this happen, I will say NO to

...and I will say YES to

I will stretch my musical comfort zone this week by

"Without music, life would be a mistake." – Friedrich Nietzsche

Monday

Tuesday

Wednesday

Thursday

Friday

Saturday

Sunday

# This Week's Reflections

What was a musical highlight for me this week?

What inspirations emerged from it?

This week, I listened to

In the coming week...

My musical musings could be

The one that excites me the most is

To make this happen, I will say NO to

...and I will say YES to

I will stretch my musical comfort zone this week by

"When I was 5 years old, my mother always told me that happiness was the key to life. When I went to school, they asked me what I wanted to be when I grew up. I wrote down 'happy.' They told me I didn't understand the assignment, and I told them they didn't understand life." – John Lennon

Monday

Tuesday

Wednesday

Thursday

Friday

Saturday

Sunday

This Week's Reflections

What was a musical highlight for me this week?

What inspirations emerged from it?

This week, I listened to

In the coming week...

My musical musings could be

The one that excites me the most is

To make this happen, I will say NO to

...and I will say YES to

I will stretch my musical comfort zone this week by

musiciansheartjourney.com

"Stay open and spontaneous so you can be the spark through which the universe expresses itself musically." – Anonymous

Monday

Tuesday

Wednesday

Thursday

Friday

Saturday

Sunday

This Week's Reflections

What was a musical highlight for me this week?

What inspirations emerged from it?

This week, I listened to

In the coming week...

My musical musings could be

The one that excites me the most is

To make this happen, I will say NO to

...and I will say YES to

I will stretch my musical comfort zone this week by

"When you want something, the entire universe conspires in helping you to achieve it." – Paulo Coelho, The Alchemist

Monday

Tuesday

Wednesday

Thursday

Friday

Saturday

Sunday

 # This Week's Reflections

What was a musical highlight for me this week?

What inspirations emerged from it?

This week, I listened to

In the coming week...

My musical musings could be

The one that excites me the most is

To make this happen, I will say NO to

...and I will say YES to

I will stretch my musical comfort zone this week by

"It is said that music is the only language where many people can talk at once and be understood. But there are still rules for conversing. Effective jamming means knowing how to listen, when to lead, and when to follow." – Philip Toshio Sudo, Zen Guitar

Monday

Tuesday

Wednesday

Thursday

Friday

Saturday

Sunday

# This Week's Reflections

What was a musical highlight for me this week?

What inspirations emerged from it?

This week, I listened to

In the coming week...

My musical musings could be

The one that excites me the most is

To make this happen, I will say NO to

...and I will say YES to

I will stretch my musical comfort zone this week by

"In the traditions of the ancient and forgotten peoples of this world, there has always been a belief that each time the breath of a human passes through an instrument of the earth, in that moment we re-enact the most sacred, the most holy act: the union between heaven and earth." – Gregg Braden

Monday

Tuesday

Wednesday

Thursday

Friday

Saturday

Sunday

This Week's Reflections

What was a musical highlight for me this week?

What inspirations emerged from it?

This week, I listened to

In the coming week...

My musical musings could be

The one that excites me the most is

To make this happen, I will say NO to

...and I will say YES to

I will stretch my musical comfort zone this week by

"If you fail to plan, you plan to fail." – Benjamin Franklin

Monday

Tuesday

Wednesday

Thursday

Friday

Saturday

Sunday

# This Week's Reflections

What was a musical highlight for me this week?

What inspirations emerged from it?

This week, I listened to

In the coming week...

My musical musings could be

The one that excites me the most is

To make this happen, I will say NO to

...and I will say YES to

I will stretch my musical comfort zone this week by

www.ingramcontent.com/pod-product-compliance
Lightning Source LLC
Chambersburg PA
CBHW081407080526
44589CB00016B/2490